Serenity

Peaceful Promises
from God's Word

Dugan, Inc. • Gordonsville, TN 38563

This book is dedicated to Arnold Dugan, Sr.—a man of strength, honor, dedication and generosity—the man who taught me to accept God's promises.

FOREWORD

SERENITY! During our times of trouble and trial, serenity is what we seek for the most. The "Peace that Passeth all understanding" is our ultimate goal.

Through His Promises, we have been given, as heirs, the distinct access to all that He is and He assures us of this through His Word. The following Promises have been compiled to assure each of us of God's provisions to us as Children of God. In times of hurting or worry, times of temptation or powerlessness, He has given us access to peace and serenity in a way which the world does not know.

As a believer in Jesus Christ, these Promises are for you. May God bless you as you accept them. We, at Dugan Publishers, pray you will experience His serenity through these, His Promises to you.

RESOURCE GUIDE

SECTION I - FEELINGS

SECTIONS I & II

FEELINGS AND CONSIDERATIONS

Each one of us has feelings which affect us in many different ways. Often, those feelings cause us to lose our fellowship with friends and loved ones, but most important, there are times when our feelings cause us to lose our fellowship with our Lord and Master, Jesus Christ. When this happens, it is then we need to evaluate our relationship with Him and rediscover who He is in our lives.

1

ANGRY

The Scriptures talk openly about Anger and its effect on our lives. The following Promises From God's Word indicate to us a loving God as well as how we should conduct ourselves and our response concerning our own anger. Read these words and meditate on them to discover God's view of anger and what our options are when we become angry.

... : but thou art a God ready to pardon, gracious and merciful, slow to anger, and of great kindness, and forsookest them not. Nehemia 9:17b

For his anger endureth but a moment; in his favour is life: weeping may endure for a night, but joy cometh in the morning. Psalm 30:5

Cease from anger, and forsake wrath: fret not thyself in any wise to do evil. Psalm 37:8

The Lord is gracious, and full of compassion; slow to anger, and of great mercy. Psalm 145:8

He that is soon angry dealeth foolishly: and a man of wicked devices is hated. Proverbs 14:17

A soft answer turneth away wrath: but grievous words stir up anger. Proverbs 15:1

A wrathful man stirreth up strife: but he that is slow to anger appeaseth strife.
Proverbs 15:18

He that is slow to anger is better than the mighty; and he that ruleth his spirit than he that taketh a city. Proverbs 16:32

The discretion of a man deferreth his anger; and it is his glory to pass over a transgression. Proverbs 19:11

It is better to dwell in the wilderness, than with a contentious and an angry woman. Proverbs 21:19

Make no friendship with an angry man; and with a furious man thou shalt not go: Lest thou learn his ways, and get a snare to thy soul. Proverbs 22:24, 25

If thine enemy be hungry, give him bread to eat; and if he be thirsty, give him water to drink: For thou shalt heap coals of fire upon his head, and the Lord shall reward thee. Proverbs 25:21, 22

An angry man stirreth up strife, and a furious man aboundeth in transgression. Proverbs 29:22

Be not hasty in thy spirit to be angry: for anger resteth in the bosom of fools. Ecclesiastes 7:9

But I say unto you, That whosoever is angry with his brother without a cause shall be in danger of the judgment: and whosoever shall say to his brother, Raca, shall be in danger of the council: but whosoever shall say, Thou fool, shall be in danger of hell fire. Matthew 5:22

Dearly beloved, avenge not yourselves, but rather give place unto wrath: for it is written, Vengeance is mine; I will repay, saith the Lord. Therefore if thine enemy hunger, feed him; if he thirst, give him drink: for in so doing thou shalt heap coals of fire on his head. Be not overcome of evil, but overcome evil with good. Romans 12:19-21

Be ye angry, and sin not: let not the sun go down upon your wrath: Ephesians 4:26

Let all bitterness, and wrath, and

anger, and clamour, and evil speaking, be put away from you, with all malice: And be ye kind one to another, tenderhearted, forgiving one another, even as God for Christ's sake hath forgiven you. Ephesians 4:31, 32

But now ye also put off all these; anger, wrath, malice, blasphemy, filthy communication out of your mouth. Colossians 3:8

Fathers, provoke not your children to anger, lest they be discouraged. Colossians 3:21

Wherefore, my beloved brethren,

let every man be swift to hear, slow to speak, slow to wrath: For the wrath of man worketh not the righteousness of God. James 1:19, 20

2

GUILTY

Guilt is used so often by the enemy of our soul to convince us that we can do nothing right and that we are without merit. What a terrible cross for us to bear unnecessarily as we go through life. We must keep in mind the following promises and instructions given expressly to us by our Lord for times such as these. Some of these verses will show us what to do with real guilt and others will show us what to do when the guilt we feel is unfounded.

For if ye turn again unto the Lord, your brethren and your children shall find compassion before them that lead them captive, so that they shall come again into this land: for the Lord your God is gracious and merciful, and will not turn away his face from you, if ye return unto him. II Chronicles 30:9

Blessed is he whose transgression is forgiven, whose sin is covered. Psalm 32:1

I acknowledged my sin unto thee, and mine iniquity have I not hid. I said, I will confess my transgressions unto the Lord; and thou forgavest the iniquity of my sin. Selah. Psalm 32:5

He hath not dealt with us after our sins; nor rewarded us according to our iniquities. Psalm 103:10

As far as the east is from the west, so far hath he removed our transgressions from us. Psalm 103:12

I, even I, am he that blotteth out thy transgressions for mine own sake, and will not remember thy sins. Isaiah 43:25

Let the wicked forsake his way, and the unrighteous man his thoughts: and let him return unto the Lord, and he will have mercy upon him; and to our God, for he will abundantly pardon. Isaiah 55:7

And they shall teach no more every man his neighbour, and every man his brother, saying, Know the Lord: for they shall all know me, from the least of them unto the greatest of them, saith the Lord; for I will forgive their iniquity, and I will remember their sin no more. Jeremiah 31:34

For God sent not his Son into the world to condemn the world; but that the world through him might be saved. He that believeth on him is not condemned: but he that believeth not is condemned already, because he hath not believed in the name of the only begotten Son of God. John 3:17, 18

Verily, verily, I say unto you, He that heareth my word, and believeth on him that sent me, hath everlasting life, and shall not come into condemnation; but is passed from death unto life. John 5:24

When Jesus had lifted up himself, and saw none but the woman, he said unto her, Woman, where are those thine accusers? hath no man condemned thee? She said, No man, Lord. And Jesus said unto her,

Neither do I condemn thee: go, and sin no more. John 8:10, 11

And herein do I exercise myself, to have always a conscience void of offence toward God, and toward men. Acts 24:16

There is therefore now no condemnation to them which are in Christ Jesus, who walk not after the flesh, but after the Spirit. Romans 8:1

Therefore if any man be in Christ, he is a new creature: old things are passed away; behold, all things are become new. II Corinthians 5:17

Now the end of the commandment is charity out of a pure heart, and of a good conscience, and of faith unfeigned: I Timothy 1:5

For I will be merciful to their unrighteousness, and their sins and their iniquities will I remember no more. Hebrews 8:12

Let us draw near with a true heart in full assurance of faith, having our hearts sprinkled from an evil conscience, and our bodies washed with pure water. Hebrews 10:22

If we confess our sins, he is faithful and just to forgive us our sins, and to cleanse us from all unrighteousness. I John 1:9

For if our heart condemn us, God is greater than our heart, and knoweth all things. I John 3:20

And Zaccaeus stood, and said unto the Lord; Behold, Lord, the half of my goods I give to the poor; and if I have taken any thing from any man by false accusation, I restore him fourfold. Luke 19:8

Submit yourselves therefore to God. Resist the devil, and he will flee from you. Draw nigh to God, and he will draw nigh to you. Cleanse your hands, ye sinners; and purify your

hearts, ye double-minded.   James
4:7,8

Behold, we count them happy
which endure. Ye have heard of the
patience of Job, and have seen the
end of the Lord; that the Lord is very
pitiful, and of tender mercy. James
5:11

And I heard a loud voice saying in
heaven, Now is come salvation, and
strength, and the kingdom of our
God, and the power of his Christ: for
the accuser of our brethren is cast
down, which accused them before our
God day and night.   And they
overcame him by the blood of the
Lamb, and by the word of their
testimony; and they loved not their
lives unto the death.   Revelation
12:10-11

3

HURT

There are times when each one of us has been hurt by the actions or inactions of another. Often, these feelings of hurt are experienced in our relationships with Christian brothers and sisters. Sometimes we are hurt by the actions of those in our home, school, office or other place of work and we need some solace or, better yet, a "balm" or ointment to help us through this difficult time. Sometimes we are hurt when we are doing what is right. Even so, take solace in the following verses.

Yea, let none that wait on thee be ashamed: let them be ashamed which transgress without cause. Psalm 25:3

Blessed are they which are persecuted for righteousness' sake: for theirs is the kingdom of heaven. Matthew 5:10

Blessed are ye, when men shall revile you, and persecute you, and shall say all manner of evil against you falsely, for my sake. Matthew 5:11

Rejoice, and be exceeding glad: for great is your reward in heaven: for so persecuted they the prophets which were before you. Matthew 5:12

But I say unto you, Love your enemies, bless them that curse you, do good to them that hate you, and pray for them which despitefully use you, and persecute you; Matthew 5:44

For if ye forgive men their trespasses, your heavenly Father will also forgive you: Matthew 6:14

But when they shall lead you, and deliver you up, take no thought beforehand what ye shall speak, neither do ye premeditate: but whatsoever shall be given you in that hour, that speak ye: for it is not ye that speak, but the Holy Ghost. Mark 13:11

And ye shall be hated of all men for my name's sake: but he that shall endure unto the end, the same shall be saved. Mark 13:13

Dearly beloved, avenge not yourselves, but rather give place unto wrath: for it is written, Vengeance is mine; I will repay, saith the Lord. Romans 12:19

Be not overcome of evil, but

overcome evil with good. Romans 12:21

Now therefore there is utterly a fault among you, because ye go to law one with another. Why do ye not rather take wrong? why do ye not rather suffer yourselves to be defrauded? I Corinthians 6:7

We are troubled on every side, yet not distressed; we are perplexed, but not in despair; Persecuted, but not forsaken; cast down, but not destroyed; II Corinthians 4:8-9

Let all bitterness, and wrath, and anger, and clamour, and evil speaking, be put away from you, with all malice: And be ye kind one to another, tenderhearted, forgiving one another, even as God for Christ's sake hath forgiven you. Ephesians 4:31

For we know him that hath said, Vengeance belongeth unto me, I will recompense, saith the Lord. And again, The Lord shall judge his people. Hebrews 10:30

For this is thankworthy, if a man for conscience toward God endure grief, suffering wrongfully. For what glory is it, if, when ye be buffeted for your faults, ye shall take it patiently? but if, when ye do well, and suffer for it, ye take it patiently, this is acceptable with God. I Peter 2:19

For even hereunto were ye called: because Christ also suffered for us, leaving us an example, that ye should follow his steps: Who did no sin, neither was guile found in his mouth: Who, when he was reviled, reviled not again; when he suffered, he threatened not; but committed himself to him that judgeth righteously: I Peter 2:21-22

Not rendering evil for evil, or railing for railing: but contrariwise blessing; knowing that ye are thereunto called, that ye should inherit a blessing. For he that will love life, and see good days, let him refrain his tongue from evil, and his lips that they speak no guile: I Peter 3:9-10

But and if ye suffer for righteousness' sake, happy are ye: and be not afraid of their terror, neither be troubled; I Peter 3:14

Beloved, think it not strange concerning the fiery trial which is to try you, as though some strange thing happened unto you: But rejoice, inasmuch as ye are partakers of Christ's sufferings; that, when his glory shall be revealed, ye may be glad also with exceeding joy. If ye be reproached for the name of Christ, happy are ye; for the spirit of glory and of God resteth upon you: on their part he is evil spoken of, but on your part he is glorified. I Peter 4:12-14

Yet if any man suffer as a Christian, let him not be ashamed; but let him glorify God on this behalf. I Peter 4:16

4

SAD

Sadness in today's world is amazingly common and there is much to be sad about. With the uncertainties which surround us and events which happen to us, we all feel sad at times and need to be reminded that God knows us and cares for us. There is no sin in sadness, but dwelling on it may cause us to fall into sin. God's promises bring us comfort in the midst of our sadness.

Though he slay me, yet will I trust in him: but I will maintain mine own ways before him. Job 13:15

But he knoweth the way that I take: when he hath tried me, I shall come forth as gold. Job 23:10

For his anger endureth but a moment; in his favour is life: weeping may endure for a night, but joy cometh in the morning. Psalm 30:5

I will be glad and rejoice in thy mercy: for thou hast considered my trouble; thou hast known my soul in adversities; Psalm 31:7

The Lord upholdeth all that fall, and raiseth up all those that be bowed down. Psalm 145:14

Surely he hath borne our griefs, and carried our sorrows: yet we did esteem him stricken, smitten of God, and afflicted. Isaiah 53:4

For ye shall go out with joy, and be led forth with peace: the mountains and the hills shall break forth before you into singing, and all the trees of the field shall clap their hands. Isaiah 55:12

The Lord is my portion, saith my soul; therefore will I hope in him. Lamentations 3:24

Verily, verily, I say unto you, That ye shall weep and lament, but the world shall rejoice: and ye shall be sorrowful, but your sorrow shall be turned into joy. John 16:20

The Spirit itself beareth witness with our spirit, that we are the children of God: And if children, then heirs; heirs of God, and joint-heirs with Christ; if so be that we suffer with him, that we may be also glorified together. For I reckon that the sufferings of this present time are not worthy to be compared with the glory which shall be revealed in us. Romans 8:16-18

Likewise the Spirit also helpeth our infirmities: for we know not what we should pray for as we ought: but the Spirit itself maketh intercession for us with groanings which cannot be uttered. And he that searcheth the hearts knoweth what is the mind of the Spirit, because he maketh intercession for the saints according to the will of God. And we know that all things work together for good to them that love God, to them who are the called according to his purpose. Romans 8:26-28

For our light affliction, which is

but for a moment, worketh for us a far more exceeding and eternal weight of glory; II Corinthians 4:17

That I may know him, and the power of his resurrection, and the fellowship of his sufferings, being made conformable unto his death; Philippians 3:10

Rejoice in the Lord alway: and again I say, Rejoice. Philippians 4:4

For God hath not appointed us to wrath, but to obtain salvation by our Lord Jesus Christ, Who died for us, that, whether we wake or sleep, we should live together with him.

Wherefore comfort yourselves together, and edify one another, even as also ye do. I Thessalonians 5:9-11

In every thing give thanks: for this is the will of God in Christ Jesus concerning you. I Thessalonians 5:18

5

THREATENED

There are times when we feel our life is being threatened and, there may well be times when this is true. Even when it isn't our very life, we do often feel threatened by situations or people and we don't quite know what our response is to be. It is in times like these that we need to renew our trust and dependence on the Lord Jesus, rather than on the people or circumstances which cause us to fear. When there is a feeling of being threatened, it behooves us to read and memorize as many of these promises as possible.

And they that know thy name will put their trust in thee: for thou, Lord, hast not forsaken them that seek thee. Psalm 9:10

When he maketh inquisition for blood, he remembereth them: he forgetteth not the cry of the humble. Psalm 9:12

I will call upon the Lord, who is worthy to be praised: so shall I be saved from mine enemies. Psalm 18:3

Thou art my hiding place; thou shalt preserve me from trouble; thou shalt compass me about with songs of deliverance. Selah. Psalm 32:7

The Lord bringeth the counsel of the heathen to nought: he maketh the devices of the people of none effect. Psalm 33:10

I sought the Lord, and he heard me, and delivered me from all my fears. Psalm 34:4

God is our refuge and strength, a very present help in trouble. Psalm 46:1

Offer unto God thanksgiving; and pay thy vows unto the most High: And call upon me in the day of trouble: I will deliver thee, and thou shalt glorify me. Psalm 50:14-15

When I cry unto thee, then shall mine enemies turn back: this I know; for God is for me. Psalm 56:9

He shall cover thee with his feathers, and under his wings shalt thou trust: his truth shall be thy shield and buckler. Thou shalt not be afraid for the terror by night; nor for the arrow that flieth by day; Psalm 91:4-5

There shall no evil befall thee, neither shall any plague come nigh thy dwelling. For he shall give his angels charge over thee, to keep thee in all thy ways. They shall bear thee up in their hands, lest thou dash thy foot against a stone. Psalm 91:10-12

Because he hath set his love upon me, therefore will I deliver him: I will set him on high, because he hath known my name. He shall call upon me, and I will answer him: I will be with him in trouble; I will deliver him, and honour him. Psalm 91:14-15

I called upon the Lord in distress: the Lord answered me, and set me in a large place. Psalm 118:5

In the day when I cried thou answeredst me, and strengthenedst me with strength in my soul. Psalm 138:3

When a man's ways please the Lord, he maketh even his enemies to be at peace with him. Proverb 16:7

Fear thou not; for I am with thee: be not dismayed; for I am thy God: I will strengthen thee; yea, I will help thee; yea, I will uphold thee with the right hand of my righteousness. Isaiah 41:10

No weapon that is formed against thee shall prosper; and every tongue that shall rise against thee in judgment thou shalt condemn. This is the heritage of the servants of the Lord, and their righteousness is of me, saith the Lord. Isaiah 54:17

But I will deliver thee in that day, saith the Lord: and thou shalt not be given into the hand of the men of whom thou art afraid. Jeremiah 39:17

And I say unto you my friends, Be not afraid of them that kill the body, and after that have no more that they can do. Luke 12:4

And I give unto them eternal life; and they shall never perish, neither shall any man pluck them out of my hand. John 10:28

So that we may boldly say, The Lord is my helper, and I will not fear what man shall do unto me. Hebrews 13:6

6

TROUBLED

There is nothing like a troubled spirit within us to keep us awake at night or cause anxiety during the day. We tend to dwell on the trouble rather than on the Lord who cares for us so much and desires for us to take our troubles to Him. It is for these times He has promised us peace for our soul and that peace comes truly from His Word. Take these promises and let them speak to your heart and spirit during times of trouble as Jesus is the "bridge over troubled water" and "He will see you through."

Though I walk in the midst of trouble, thou wilt revive me: thou shalt stretch forth thine hand against the wrath of mine enemies, and thy right hand shall save me. Psalm 138:7

Therefore I say unto you, Take no thought for your life, what ye shall eat, or what ye shall drink; nor yet for your body, what ye shall put on. Is not the life more than meat, and the body than raiment? Behold the fowls of the air: for they sow not, neither do they reap, nor gather into barns; yet your heavenly Father feedeth them. Are ye not much better than they? Which of you by taking thought can add one cubit unto his stature? And why take ye thought for raiment? Consider the lilies of the field, how they grow; they toil not, neither do they spin: And yet I say unto you, That even Solomon in all his glory was not arrayed like one of these. Wherefore, if God so clothe the grass of the field, which to day is, and to morrow is cast into the oven, shall he not much more clothe you, O ye of little faith? Therefore take no thought, saying, What shall we eat? or, What shall we drink? or, Wherewithal shall we be clothed? (For after all these things do the Gentiles seek:) for your heavenly Father knoweth that ye have need of all these things. But seek ye first the kingdom of God, and his righteousness; and all these things shall be added unto you. Take therefore no thought for the morrow: for the morrow shall take thought for the things of itself. Sufficient unto the day is the evil thereof. Matthew 6:25-34

Ask, and it shall be given you; seek, and ye shall find; knock, and it shall be opened unto you: For every one that asketh receiveth; and he that seeketh findeth; and to him that knocketh it shall be opened. Or what man is there of you, whom if his son ask bread, will he give him a stone? Or if he ask a fish, will he give him a serpent? If ye then, being evil, know how to give good gifts unto your children, how much more shall your Father which is in heaven give good things to them that ask him? Matthew 7:7-11

Fear not, little flock; for it is your Father's good pleasure to give you the kingdom. Luke 12:32

Let not your heart be troubled: ye believe in God, believe also in me. John 14:1

Peace I leave with you, my peace I give unto you: not as the world giveth, give I unto you. Let not your heart be troubled, neither let it be afraid. John 14:27

Blessed be God, even the Father of our Lord Jesus Christ, the Father of mercies, and the God of all comfort; Who comforteth us in all our tribulation, that we may be able to comfort them which are in any trouble, by the comfort wherewith we ourselves are comforted of God. II Corinthians 1:3-4

We are troubled on every side, yet not distressed; we are perplexed, but not in despair; Persecuted, but not forsaken; cast down, but not destroyed; II Corinthians 4:8-9

Be careful for nothing; but in every thing by prayer and supplication with thanksgiving let your requests be made known unto God. And the peace of God, which passeth all understanding, shall keep your hearts and minds through Christ Jesus. Philippians 4:6-7

Let us therefore come boldly unto the throne of grace, that we may obtain mercy, and find grace to help in time of need. Hebrews 4:16

7

USELESS

Feeling useless is one of the most depressing of all feelings. We get this feeling in the very pit of our stomach that not only are we useless, but it is useless to try to do anything. It leaves us paralyzed and without direction. God doesn't look on us that way, but we see ourselves in this self made mirror and need God to give us new purpose and direction. It is exactly that which we can gain from His promises to us.

Ye are my witnesses, saith the Lord, and my servant whom I have chosen: that ye may know and believe me, and understand that I am he: before me there was no God formed, neither shall there be after me. Isaiah 43:10

The Lord hath brought forth our righteousness: come, and let us declare in Zion the work of the Lord our God. Jeremiah 51:10

And whosoever shall give to drink unto one of these little ones a cup of cold water only in the name of a disciple, verily I say unto you, he shall in no wise lose his reward.

And all things are of God, who hath reconciled us to himself by Jesus Christ, and hath given to us the ministry of reconciliation; II Corinthians 5:18

Now then we are ambassadors for Christ, as though God did beseech you by us: we pray you in Christ's stead, be ye reconciled to God. II Corinthians 5:20

And what agreement hath the temple of God with idols? for ye are the temple of the living God; as God hath said, I will dwell in them, and walk in them; and I will be their God, and they shall be my people. II Corinthians 6:16

And because ye are sons, God hath sent forth the Spirit of his Son into your hearts, crying, Abba, Father.
Wherefore thou art no more a servant, but a son; and if a son, then an heir of God through Christ. Galatians 4:6-7

For we are his workmanship, created in Christ Jesus unto good works, which God hath before ordained that we should walk in them. Ephesians 2:10

But ye are a chosen generation, a royal priesthood, an holy nation, a peculiar people; that ye should shew forth the praises of him who hath called you out of darkness into his marvellous light: I Peter 2:9

Beloved, now are we the sons of God, and it doth not yet appear what we shall be: but we know that, when he shall appear, we shall be like him; for we shall see him as he is. I John 3:2

And from Jesus Christ, who is the faithful witness, and the first begotten of the dead, and the prince of the kings of the earth. Unto him that loved us, and washed us from our sins in his own blood, And hath

made us kings and priests unto God
and his Father; to him be glory and
dominion for ever and ever. Amen.
Revelation 1:5-6

And they sung a new song,
saying, Thou art worthy to take the
book, and to open the seals thereof:
for thou wast slain, and hast
redeemed us to God by thy blood out
of every kindred, and tongue, and
people, and nation; And hast made
us unto our God kings and priests:
and we shall reign on the earth.
Revelation 5:9-10

8

WORRIED

Worry is often self induced, but, nevertheless, worry is real. We have a tendency to convince ourselves that everything is out of control and, therefore, we must worry. It is easy for us to forget that we are not in charge, but that our Loving Heavenly Father is and He has our best interest at heart. Our faith cannot be based on our feelings, but on God's goodness. It is, therefore, necessary, to remind ourselves that God is the One who takes care of us. These promises of God certainly are written for our use today.

I will both lay me down in peace, and sleep: for thou, Lord, only makest me dwell in safety. Psalm 4:8

What man is he that feareth the Lord? him shall he teach in the way that he shall choose. His soul shall dwell at ease; and his seed shall inherit the earth. Psalm 25:12-13

Thou art my hiding place; thou shalt preserve me from trouble; thou shalt compass me about with songs of deliverance. Selah. Psalm 32:7

Cast thy burden upon the Lord, and he shall sustain thee: he shall never suffer the righteous to be moved. Psalm 55:22

He that dwelleth in the secret place of the most High shall abide under the shadow of the Almighty. Psalm 91:1

I will say of the Lord, He is my refuge and my fortress: my God; in him will I trust. Psalm 91:2

Thou shalt tread upon the lion and adder: the young lion and the dragon shalt thou trample under feet. Because he hath set his love upon me, therefore will I deliver him: I will set him on high, because he hath known my name. He shall call upon me, and I will answer him: I will be with him in trouble; I will deliver him, and honour him. Psalm 91:13-15

Thou wilt keep him in perfect peace, whose mind is stayed on thee: because he trusteth in thee. Isaiah 26:3

Therefore I say unto you, Take no thought for your life, what ye shall eat, or what ye shall drink; nor yet for your body, what ye shall put on. Is not the life more than meat, and the body than raiment? Matthew

Wherefore, if God so clothe the grass of the field, which to day is, and to morrow is cast into the oven, shall he not much more clothe you, O ye of little faith? Matthew 6:30

But seek ye first the kingdom of God, and his righteousness; and all these things shall be added unto you. Take therefore no thought for the morrow: for the morrow shall take thought for the things of itself. Sufficient unto the day is the evil thereof. Matthew 6:33-34

Let not your heart be troubled: ye believe in God, believe also in me. **John 14:1**

Be careful for nothing; but in every thing by prayer and supplication with thanksgiving let your requests be made known unto God. And the peace of God, which passeth all understanding, shall keep your hearts and minds through Christ Jesus. **Philippians 4:6-7**

But my God shall supply all your need according to his riches in glory by Christ Jesus. **Philippians 4:19**

And let the peace of God rule in your hearts, to the which also ye are called in one body; and be ye thankful. Colossians 3:15

If any of you lack wisdom, let him ask of God, that giveth to all men liberally, and upbraideth not; and it shall be given him. James 1:5

Casting all your care upon him; for he careth for you. I Peter 5:7

9

FORSAKEN

To feel forsaken is as near suicide as a person can get. We fall into this pit of self destruction, thinking that everyone has left us and we are all alone. What a serious lie for us to believe. Yes, we can be forsaken by friends and even family, but never by God. He has promised to be with us always. God is not going to forsake us as He is too loving to even consider such a move, while we only think we have been left.

Read these promises and believe them and then there can be no doubt as to God's continued care for each of us.

(For the Lord thy God is a merciful God;) he will not forsake thee, neither destroy thee, nor forget the covenant of thy fathers which he sware unto them. Deuteronomy 4:31

Know therefore that the Lord thy God, he is God, the faithful God, which keepeth covenant and mercy with them that love him and keep his commandments to a thousand generations; Deuteronomy 7:9

Be strong and of a good courage, fear not, nor be afraid of them: for the Lord thy God, he it is that doth go with thee; he will not fail thee, nor forsake thee. Deuteronomy 31:6

For the Lord will not forsake his people for his great name's sake: because it hath pleased the Lord to make you his people. I Samuel 12:22

And they that know thy name will put their trust in thee: for thou, Lord, hast not forsaken them that seek thee. Psalm 9:10

For thou wilt not leave my soul in hell; neither wilt thou suffer thine Holy One to see corruption. Psalm 16:10

When my father and my mother forsake me, then the Lord will take me up. Psalm 27:10

I have been young, and now am old; yet have I not seen the righteous forsaken, nor his seed begging bread. Psalm 37:25

Because he hath set his love upon me, therefore will I deliver him: I will set him on high, because he hath known my name. He shall call upon me, and I will answer him: I will be with him in trouble; I will deliver him, and honour him. Psalm 91:14-15

For the Lord will not cast off his people, neither will he forsake his inheritance. Psalm 94:14

He will swallow up death in victory; and the Lord God will wipe away tears from off all faces; and the rebuke of his people shall he take away from off all the earth: for the Lord hath spoken it. Isaiah 25:8

When the poor and needy seek water, and there is none, and their tongue faileth for thirst, I the Lord will hear them, I the God of Israel will not forsake them. Isaiah 41:17

Can a woman forget her sucking child, that she should not have compassion on the son of her womb? yea, they may forget, yet will I not forget thee. Behold, I have graven thee upon the palms of my hands; thy walls are continually before me. Isaiah 49:15

For thy Maker is thine husband; the Lord of hosts is his name; and thy Redeemer the Holy One of Israel; The God of the whole earth shall he be called. For the Lord hath called thee as a woman forsaken and grieved in spirit, and a wife of youth, when thou wast refused, saith thy God. For a small moment have I forsaken thee; but with great mercies will I gather thee. In a little wrath I hid my face from thee for a moment; but with everlasting kindness will I have mercy on thee, saith the Lord thy Redeemer. For this is as the waters of Noah unto me: for as I have sworn that the waters of Noah should no more go over the earth; so have I sworn that I would not be wroth with thee, nor rebuke thee. For the mountains shall depart, and the hills be removed; but my kindness shall not depart from thee, neither shall the covenant of my peace be removed, saith the Lord that hath mercy on thee. O thou afflicted, tossed with tempest, and not comforted, behold, I will lay thy stones with fair colours, and lay thy foundations with sapphires. And I will make thy windows of agates, and thy gates of carbuncles, and all thy borders of pleasant stones. And all thy children shall be taught of the Lord; and great shall be the peace of thy children. In righteousness shalt thou be established: thou shalt be far from oppression; for thou shalt not fear: and from terror; for it shall not come near thee. Behold, they shall surely gather together, but not by me: whosoever shall gather together against thee shall fall for thy sake. Isaiah 54:5-15

Thou shalt no more be termed Forsaken; neither shall thy land any more be termed Desolate: but thou shalt be called Hephzi-bah, and thy land Beulah: for the Lord delighteth in thee, and thy land shall be married. Isaiah 62:4

Teaching them to observe all things whatsoever I have commanded you: and, lo, I am with you alway, even unto the end of the world. Amen. Matthew 28:20

All that the Father giveth me shall come to me; and him that cometh to me I will in no wise cast out. John 6:37

A woman when she is in travail hath sorrow, because her hour is come: but as soon as she is delivered of the child, she remembereth no more the anguish, for joy that a man is born into the world. And ye now therefore have sorrow: but I will see you again, and your heart shall rejoice, and your joy no man taketh from you. John 16:21-22

And we know that all things work together for good to them that love God, to them who are the called according to his purpose. For whom he did foreknow, he also did predestinate to be conformed to the image of his Son, that he might be the firstborn among many brethren. Moreover whom he did predestinate, them he also called: and whom he called, them he also justified: and whom he justified, them he also glorified. Romans 8:28-30

For now we see through a glass, darkly; but then face to face: now I know in part; but then shall I know even as also I am known. I Corinthians 13:12

Persecuted, but not forsaken; cast down, but not destroyed; II

Casting all your care upon him; for he careth for you. I Peter 5:7

Beloved, now are we the sons of God, and it doth not yet appear what we shall be: but we know that, when he shall appear, we shall be like him; for we shall see him as he is. I John 3:2

10

HOPELESS

Utter hopelessness is being reserved for Satan, his hordes and those who have rejected Jesus Christ as Savior. Although there are times when we feel hopeless in this life, we must remember this feeling is not what God has planned for us. Instead, when we feel hopeless, we can turn to the Bible, and meditate on the promises which He has given to us. It is only with this assurance that we can even begin to overcome this sense of hopeless abandon.

And thou shalt be secure, because there is hope; yea, thou shalt dig about thee, and thou shalt take thy rest in safety. Job 11:18

For the needy shall not alway be forgotten: the expectation of the poor shall not perish for ever. Psalm 9:18

Therefore my heart is glad, and my glory rejoiceth: my flesh also shall rest in hope. For thou wilt not leave my soul in hell; neither wilt thou suffer thine Holy One to see corruption. Psalm 16:9-10.

Wait on the Lord: be of good courage, and he shall strengthen thine heart: wait, I say, on the Lord. Psalm 27:14

But the salvation of the righteous is of the Lord: he is their strength in the time of trouble. Psalm 37:39

Why art thou cast down, O my soul? and why art thou disquieted within me? hope in God: for I shall yet praise him, who is the health of my countenance, and my God. Psalm 43:5

For thou art my hope, O Lord

God: thou art my trust from my youth. Psalm 71:5

By thee have I been holden up from the womb: thou art he that took me out of my mother's bowels: my praise shall be continually of thee. Psalm 71:6

Remember the word unto thy servant, upon which thou hast caused me to hope. This is my comfort in my affliction: for thy word hath quickened me. Psalm 119:49-50

My soul fainteth for thy salvation: but I hope in thy word. Psalm 119:81

I wait for the Lord, my soul doth wait, and in his word do I hope. Psalm 130:5

The hope of the righteous shall be gladness: but the expectation of the wicked shall perish. Proverb 10:28

For surely there is an end; and thine expectation shall not be cut off. Proverb 23:18

This I recall to my mind, therefore have I hope. Lamentations 3:21

It is of the Lord's mercies that we are not consumed, because his compassions fail not. They are new every morning: great is thy faithfulness. The Lord is my portion, saith my soul; therefore will I hope in him. Lamentations 3:22-24

The Lord is good unto them that wait for him, to the soul that seeketh him. Lamentations 3:25

It is good that a man should both hope and quietly wait for the salvation of the Lord. Lamentations 3:26

Turn you to the strong hold, ye prisoners of hope: even to day do I declare that I will render double unto thee; Zechariah 9:12

Therefore being justified by faith, we have peace with God through our Lord Jesus Christ: By whom also we have access by faith into this grace wherein we stand, and rejoice in hope of the glory of God. And not only so, but we glory in tribulations also: knowing that tribulation worketh patience; And patience, experience; and experience, hope: And hope maketh not ashamed; because the love of God is shed abroad in our hearts by the Holy Ghost which is given unto us. Romans 5:1-5

For we are saved by hope: but hope that is seen is not hope: for what a man seeth, why doth he yet hope for? Romans 8:24

For whatsoever things were written aforetime were written for our learning, that we through patience and comfort of the scriptures might have hope. Romans 15:4

Now the God of hope fill you with all joy and peace in believing, that ye may abound in hope, through the power of the Holy Ghost. Romans 15:13

For our light affliction, which is but for a moment, worketh for us a far more exceeding and eternal weight of glory; While we look not at the things which are seen, but at the things which are not seen: for the things which are seen are temporal; but the things which are not seen are eternal. II Corinthians 4:17-18

11

LONELY

The world is often a lonely place. We can find ourselves alone in large crowds and in private rooms. Noone seems to care nor does anyone call or offer us a listening ear. We feel that we are not wanted nor cared for and our loneliness sinks deeper and deeper into our inner being. But, be of good cheer, God has not left us alone, but rather has made provisions to heal our loneliness through His promises and we can take Him at His Word. These promises are written to us for these times of loneliness.

The eternal God is thy refuge, and underneath are the everlasting arms: and he shall thrust out the enemy from before thee; and shall say, Destroy them. Deuteronomy 33:27

The Lord also will be a refuge for the oppressed, a refuge in times of trouble. Psalm 9:9

And they that know thy name will put their trust in thee: for thou, Lord, hast not forsaken them that seek thee. Psalm 9:10

I will be glad and rejoice in thy mercy: for thou hast considered my trouble; thou hast known my soul in adversities; Psalm 31:7

God is our refuge and strength, a very present help in trouble. Psalm 46:1

Cast thy burden upon the Lord, and he shall sustain thee: he shall never suffer the righteous to be moved. Psalm 55:22

Truly my soul waiteth upon God: from him cometh my salvation. He only is my rock and my salvation;

he is my defence; I shall not be greatly moved. Psalm 62:1-2

God setteth the solitary in families: he bringeth out those which are bound with chains: but the rebellious dwell in a dry land. Psalm 68:6

Like as a father pitieth his children, so the Lord pitieth them that fear him. Psalm 103:13

Unto the upright there ariseth light in the darkness: he is gracious, and full of compassion, and righteous. Psalm 112:4

He healeth the broken in heart, and bindeth up their wounds. Psalm 147:3

For the people shall dwell in Zion at Jerusalem: thou shalt weep no more: he will be very gracious unto thee at the voice of thy cry; when he shall hear it, he will answer thee. Isaiah 30:19

Fear thou not; for I am with thee: be not dismayed; for I am thy God: I will strengthen thee; yea, I will help thee; yea, I will uphold thee with the right hand of my righteousness. Isaiah 41:10

In all their affliction he was afflicted, and the angel of his presence saved them: in his love and in his pity he redeemed them; and he bare them, and carried them all the days of old. Isaiah 63:9

The Lord is good, a strong hold in the day of trouble; and he knoweth them that trust in him. Nahum 1:7

Teaching them to observe all things whatsoever I have commanded you: and, lo, I am with you alway, even unto the end of the world. Amen. Matthew 28:20

Let not your heart be troubled:

ye believe in God, believe also in me.
John 14:1

I will not leave you comfortless:
I will come to you. John 14:18

Who shall separate us from the
love of Christ? shall tribulation, or
distress, or persecution, or famine, or
nakedness, or peril, or sword?
Romans 8:35

For I am persuaded, that
neither death, nor life, nor angels,
nor principalities, nor powers, nor
things present, nor things to come,
Nor height, nor depth, nor any other
creature, shall be able to separate us

from the love of God, which is in Christ Jesus our Lord. Romans 8:38-39

Let your conversation be without covetousness; and be content with such things as ye have: for he hath said, I will never leave thee, nor forsake thee. Hebrews 13:5

Casting all your care upon him; for he careth for you. I Peter 5:7

12

TEMPTED

We may be tempted to give in to addictions, immoral behavior, financial or other sins, but God is never the one who tempts us to do evil. We can be certain that if we are tempted, the temptation comes from the enemy of our souls or from our own desires, lusts or ambitions. When we are tempted, we do, however, have an answer which strengthens us. That is God's Word for our lives. The following promises of God are written to us for our benefit when temptation overcomes us, no matter from what source or in which manner.

Blessed is the man that walketh not in the counsel of the ungodly, nor standeth in the way of sinners, nor sitteth in the seat of the scornful. But his delight is in the law of the Lord; and in his law doth he meditate day and night. And he shall be like a tree planted by the rivers of water, that bringeth forth his fruit in his season; his leaf also shall not wither; and whatsoever he doeth shall prosper. Psalm 1:1-3

Wherefore doth the wicked contemn God? he hath said in his heart, Thou wilt not require it. Psalm 10:13

Thy word have I hid in mine heart, that I might not sin against thee. Psalm 119:11

And the Lord said, Simon, Simon, behold, Satan hath desired to have you, that he may sift you as wheat: But I have prayed for thee, that thy faith fail not: and when thou art converted, strengthen thy brethren. Luke 22:31-32

For sin shall not have dominion over you: for ye are not under the law, but under grace. Romans 6:14

There hath no temptation taken you but such as is common to man: but God is faithful, who will not suffer you to be tempted above that ye are able; but will with the temptation also make a way to escape, that ye may be able to bear it. I Corinthians 10:13

Finally, my brethren, be strong in the Lord, and in the power of his might. Put on the whole armour of God, that ye may be able to stand against the wiles of the devil. Ephesians 6:10-11

Above all, taking the shield of faith, wherewith ye shall be able to quench all the fiery darts of the wicked. Ephesians 6:16

For in that he himself hath suffered being tempted, he is able to succour them that are tempted. Hebrews 2:18

For we have not an high priest which cannot be touched with the feeling of our infirmities; but was in all points tempted like as we are, yet without sin. Let us therefore come boldly unto the throne of grace, that we may obtain mercy, and find grace to help in time of need. Hebrews 4:15-16

My brethren, count it all joy when ye fall into divers temptations;

Knowing this, that the trying of your faith worketh patience. James 1:2-3

Blessed is the man that endureth temptation: for when he is tried, he shall receive the crown of life, which the Lord hath promised to them that love him. James 1:12

Let no man say when he is tempted, I am tempted of God: for God cannot be tempted with evil, neither tempteth he any man: But every man is tempted, when he is drawn away of his own lust, and enticed. James 1:13-14

Submit yourselves therefore to

God. Resist the devil, and he will flee from you. James 4:7

Wherein ye greatly rejoice, though now for a season, if need be, ye are in heaviness through manifold temptations: That the trial of your faith, being much more precious than of gold that perisheth, though it be tried with fire, might be found unto praise and honour and glory at the appearing of Jesus Christ: I Peter 1:6-7

Be sober, be vigilant; because your adversary the devil, as a roaring lion, walketh about, seeking whom he may devour: Whom resist stedfast in the faith, knowing that the same afflictions are accomplished in your brethren that are in the world. I

Peter 5:8-9

The Lord knoweth how to
deliver the godly out of temptations,
and to reserve the unjust unto the
day of judgment to be punished: II
Peter 2:9

Ye are of God, little children,
and have overcome them: because
greater is he that is in you, than he
that is in the world. I John 4:4

13

TIRED

There are times in everyone's life when we are simply tired - tired physically, emotionally and even sometimes spiritually. We need a "re-charge" of our batteries, but we must remember to plug into the "source." It is God's Word which is the significant source for our lives. When a good night's sleep isn't the answer for our physical condition, then, as always, the Word of God is the necessary prescription to give us our emotional rest to renew our spiritual vitality.

The righteous also shall hold on his way, and he that hath clean hands shall be stronger and stronger. Job 17:9

Thus saith the Lord, Stand ye in the ways, and see, and ask for the old paths, where is the good way, and walk therein, and ye shall find rest for your souls. But they said, We will not walk therein. Jeremiah 6:16

Come unto me, all ye that labour and are heavy laden, and I

will give you rest. Matthew 11:28

Wherefore we labour, that, whether present or absent, we may be accepted of him. II Corinthians 5:9

And let us not be weary in well doing: for in due season we shall reap, if we faint not. Galatians 6:9

For now we live, if ye stand fast in the Lord. I Thessalonians 3:8

And the Lord shall deliver me from every evil work, and will preserve me unto his heavenly kingdom: to whom be glory for ever and ever. Amen. II Timothy 4:18

For we which have believed do enter into rest, as he said, As I have sworn in my wrath, if they shall enter into my rest: although the works were finished from the foundation of the world. Hebrews 4:3

There remaineth therefore a rest to the people of God. For he that is entered into his rest, he also hath ceased from his own works, as God did from his. Let us labour therefore to enter into that rest, lest any man fall after the same example of unbelief. Hebrews 4:9-11

Now no chastening for the present seemeth to be joyous, but grievous: nevertheless afterward it yieldeth the peaceable fruit of righteousness unto them which are exercised thereby. Wherefore lift up the hands which hang down, and the feeble knees; And make straight paths for your feet, lest that which is lame be turned out of the way; but let it rather be healed. Hebrews 12:11-13

Be ye also patient; stablish your hearts: for the coming of the Lord draweth nigh. James 5:8

Take, my brethren, the prophets, who have spoken in the name of the Lord, for an example of suffering affliction, and of patience. James 5:10

Behold, we count them happy which endure. Ye have heard of the patience of Job, and have seen the end of the Lord; that the Lord is very pitiful, and of tender mercy. James 5:11

14

UNFULFILLED

This is a difficult emotion to cope with. Doing well, but not feeling fulfilled has caused many Christians to turn away from the truth, but mature Christians know that fulfillment is not a feeling, but rather a position in and with our Lord Jesus Christ. If we are "feeling" unfulfilled, it is time for us to begin to realize that our fulfillment is not in doing things, but in being children of the Living God. Therefore, we are already fulfilled in Him. Take the time necessary to review these promises and renew your sense of fulfillment in Jesus Christ.

As for me, I will behold thy face in righteousness: I shall be satisfied, when I awake, with thy likeness. Psalm 17:15

The meek shall eat and be satisfied: they shall praise the Lord that seek him: your heart shall live for ever. Psalm 22:26

Delight thyself also in the Lord; and he shall give thee the desires of thine heart. Psalm 37:4

My soul shall be satisfied as with marrow and fatness; and my mouth shall praise thee with joyful lips: When I remember thee upon my bed, and meditate on thee in the night watches. Psalm 63:5-6

For the Lord God is a sun and shield: the Lord will give grace and glory: no good thing will he withhold from them that walk uprightly. Psalm 84:11

Who satisfieth thy mouth with good things; so that thy youth is renewed like the eagle's. Psalm 103:5

For he satisfieth the longing

soul, and filleth the hungry soul with goodness. Psalm 107:9

The eyes of all wait upon thee; and thou givest them their meat in due season. Thou openest thine hand, and satisfiest the desire of every living thing. Psalm 145:15-16

But they that wait upon the Lord shall renew their strength; they shall mount up with wings as eagles; they shall run, and not be weary; and they shall walk, and not faint. Isaiah 40:31

Wherefore do ye spend money for that which is not bread? and your labour for that which satisfieth not?

hearken diligently unto me, and eat ye that which is good, and let your soul delight itself in fatness. Isaiah 55:2

And if thou draw out thy soul to the hungry, and satisfy the afflicted soul; then shall thy light rise in obscurity, and thy darkness be as the noonday: Isaiah 58:10

And the Lord shall guide thee continually, and satisfy thy soul in drought, and make fat thy bones: and thou shalt be like a watered garden, and like a spring of water, whose waters fail not. Isaiah 58:11

And I will satiate the soul of the priests with fatness, and my people shall be satisfied with my goodness, saith the Lord. Jeremiah 31:14

Yea, the Lord will answer and say unto his people, Behold, I will send you corn, and wine, and oil, and ye shall be satisfied therewith: and I will no more make you a reproach among the heathen: Joel 2:19

And ye shall eat in plenty, and be satisfied, and praise the name of the Lord your God, that hath dealt wondrously with you: and my people shall never be ashamed. Joel 2:26

Blessed are they which do hunger and thirst after righteousness: for they shall be filled. Matthew 5:6

Jesus answered and said unto her, Whosoever drinketh of this water shall thirst again: But whosoever drinketh of the water that I shall give him shall never thirst; but the water that I shall give him shall be in him a well of water springing up into everlasting life. John 4:13-14

And Jesus said unto them, I am the bread of life: he that cometh to me shall never hunger; and he that believeth on me shall never thirst. John 6:35

He that spared not his own Son, but delivered him up for us all, how shall he not with him also freely give us all things? Romans 8:32

15

POWERLESS

There is an old gospel song which rings in our ears: "I am weak, but He is strong. Jesus keep me from all wrong: I'll be satisfied as long, as I walk, let me walk close to Thee." We are powerless compared to our great our Lord; but, He gives us strength when we call on Him. With only words, He made all there is in existence. It is amazing that though we are weak and He is strong, He has invited us to partake of His strength and the following promises are

His Words of Power to us. They confirm His desire to give us strength.

But against any of the children of Israel shall not a dog move his tongue, against man or beast: that ye may know how that the Lord doth put a difference between the Egyptians and Israel. Exodus 11:7

Thy shoes shall be iron and brass; and as thy days, so shall thy strength be. Deuteronomy 33:25

God is my strength and power: and he maketh my way perfect. II Samuel 22:33

The Lord is my rock, and my fortress, and my deliverer; my God, my strength, in whom I will trust; my buckler, and the horn of my salvation, and my high tower. Psalm 18:2

The Lord is my light and my salvation; whom shall I fear? the Lord is the strength of my life; of whom shall I be afraid? Psalm 27:1

The Lord is their strength, and he is the saving strength of his anointed.
Psalm 28:8

Save thy people, and bless thine inheritance: feed them also, and lift them up for ever. Psalm 28:9

The Lord will give strength unto his people; the Lord will bless his people with peace. Psalm 29:11

But the salvation of the righteous is of the Lord: he is their strength in the time of trouble. Psalm 37:39

For the Lord shall be thy confidence, and shall keep thy foot from being taken. Proverb 3:26

The way of the Lord is strength

to the upright: but destruction shall be to the workers of iniquity. Proverb 10:29

He giveth power to the faint; and to them that have no might he increaseth strength. Isaiah 40:29

Even the youths shall faint and be weary, and the young men shall utterly fall: But they that wait upon the Lord shall renew their strength; they shall mount up with wings as eagles; they shall run, and not be weary; and they shall walk, and not faint. Isaiah 40:30-31

Fear thou not; for I am with

thee: be not dismayed; for I am thy God: I will strengthen thee; yea, I will help thee; yea, I will uphold thee with the right hand of my righteousness. Isaiah 41:10

I the Lord have called thee in righteousness, and will hold thine hand, and will keep thee, and give thee for a covenant of the people, for a light of the Gentiles; Isaiah 42:6

And he said unto me, My grace is sufficient for thee: for my strength is made perfect in weakness. Most gladly therefore will I rather glory in my infirmities, that the power of Christ may rest upon me. II Corinthians 12:9

I can do all things through Christ which strengtheneth me. Philippians 4:13

For God hath not given us the spirit of fear; but of power, and of love, and of a sound mind. II Timothy 1:7

16

CONSIDER JESUS

As the foregoing promises are certainly for us in our time of need, let's transfer our eyes unto our Savior who gives us these promises: "Looking unto Jesus, the author and finisher of our faith ..." and consider not what He can do for us, but Who He Is.

CONSIDER: He Was/Is

Obedient. Philippians 2:8

Meek and Lowly. Matthew 11:29

Guileless. I Peter 2:22

Tempted. Hebrews 4:15

Oppressed. Isaiah 53:7

Despised. Isaiah 53:3

Rejected. Isaiah 53:3

Betrayed. Matthew 27:3

Condemned. Mark 14:64

Reviled. I Peter 2:23

Scourged. John 19:1

Mocked. Matthew 27:29

Wounded. Isaiah 53:5

Bruised. Isaiah 53:5

Stricken. Isaiah 53:4

Smitten. Isaiah 53:4

Crucified. Matthew 27:35

Forsaken. Psalm 22:1

Merciful. Hebrews 2:17

Faithful. Hebrews 2:17

Holy/Harmless. Hebrews 7:26

Undefiled. Hebrews 7:26

Separate. Hebrews 7:26

Perfect. Hebrews 5:9

Glorious. Isaiah 49:5

Mighty. Isaiah 63:1

Justified. I Timothy 3:16

Exalted. Acts 2:33

Risen. Luke 24:6

Glorified. Acts 3:13

HE IS:

My Maker. Isaiah 54:5

My Well-beloved. Song of Sol. 1:13

My Savior. II Peter 3:18

My Hope. I Timothy 1:1

My Brother. Mark 3:35

My Portion. Jeremiah 10:16

My Helper. Hebrews 13:6

My Physician. Jeremiah 8:22

My Healer. Luke 9:11

My Refiner. Malachi 3:3

My Purifier. Malachi 3:3

My Lord, Master. John 13:13

My Servant. Luke 12:37

My Example. John 13:15

My Teacher. John 3:2

My Shepherd. Psalm 23:1

My Keeper. John 17:12

My Feeder. Ezekiel 34:23

My Leader. Isaiah 40:11

My Restorer. Psalm 23:3

My Resting-place. Jeremiah 50:6

My Passover. I Corinthians 5:7

My Peace. Ephesians 2:14

My Wisdom. I Corinthians 1:30

My Righteousness. I Corinthians 1:30

My Sanctification. I Corinthians 1:30

My Redemption. I Corinthians 1:30

My All in All. Colossians 3:11

Unto us a Child is born, unto us a SON is given: and his name shall be called Wonderful, Counsellor, the Mighty God, the Everlasting Father, the Prince of Peace. Isaiah 9:6.

Then he said unto them, O fools, and slow of heart to believe ALL that the Prophets have spoken!

And beginning at Moses, and ALL the Prophets, he expounded unto them in ALL the Scriptures the things concerning HIMSELF. Luke 24:25, 27.

That all should honor the SON, even as they honor the Father. He that honoreth not the SON, honoreth not the Father which has sent him. John 5:23.

17

OUR POSITION IN CHRIST

The Scriptures tell us that we are a "special" people if we know the Lord Jesus Christ as our Savior and Lord. As special people, we have been placed by God Himself into a special place in His heart and in His plan for mankind. It is with this thought in mind that the following 103 verses have been compiled to show each of us our most favored position in Christ Jesus and what it means to each of us on a daily basis. Consider your position in Christ from these

103 verses.

So you can reconfirm your own position in Christ Jesus, each verse has a space for you to sign your name. By signing your name, you are making a covenant with God and affirming your faith and belief in His Word and these Promises given to you.

1. I, _____,

am born again. I Peter 1:23

2. I, _____,

am a child of God. John 1:12

3. I, _____,

am a saint. I Corinthians 1:2

4. I, _____,

am the salt of the earth. Matthew 5:13

5. I, _____,

am the light of the world. Matthew 5:14

6. I, _____,

am a disciple because I have love for others. John 13:34-35

7. I, _____,

am protected by the power of His Name. John 17:11

8. I, _____,

am set free by the truth. John 8:31-33

9. I, _____,

am safe and secure in Christ. John
10:27-31

10. I, _____,
am kept from the evil one. John 15:17

11. I, _____,
am one with God the Father and
Jesus the Son. John 17:23

12. I, _____,
am God's gift to Christ. John 17:24

13. I, _____,
have peace with God. Romans 5:1

14. I, _____,
have been justified by faith. Romans
5:1

15. I, _____,
have access into the sphere of God's
Grace. Romans 5:2

16. I, _____,
can rejoice in trouble. Romans 5:3

17. I, _____,
have the love of God poured out in
my heart. Romans 5:5

18. I, _____,

am reigning in the life of Jesus
Christ. Romans 5:17

19. I, _____,
have been reconciled to God through
the death of Jesus. Romans 5:10

20. I, _____,
am being saved by the life of Jesus.
Romans 5:10b

21. I, _____,
have been baptized into Christ's
death. Romans 6:3

22. I, _____,
have been raised to walk in the
newness of life. Romans 6:4

23. I, _____,
have been united with Christ through
His death and resurrection. Romans
6:5

24. I, _____,
(my old self) was crucified with
Christ. Romans 6:6

25. I, _____,
am alive to God in Christ. Romans
6:11

26. I, _____,

am yielded to God. Romans 6:13

27. I, _____,

am not under the law, but under

grace. Romans 6:14

28. I, _____,

have eternal life in Christ. Romans

6:23

29. I, _____,

am free from the power of sin.

Romans 6:18

30. I, _____,

am free from condemnation. Romans
8:1

31. I, _____,
am a servant of God. Romans 6:22

32. I, _____,
have been set free from the power of
sin and am now a servant of
righteousness. Romans 6:18

33. I, _____,
am free from the vicious cycle of sin
and death. Romans 6:18

34. I, _____,

am indwelt by the Holy Spirit.
Romans 8:9

35. I, _____,
am led by the Holy Spirit. Romans
8:14

36. I, _____,
am a joint heir with Christ. Romans
8:17

37. I, _____,
am confident that all things work
together for good. Romans 8:28

38. I, _____,

am being conformed to the image of Christ. Romans 8:29

39. I, _____,
know the Holy Spirit helps my infirmities. Romans 8:26

40. I, _____,
know the Holy Spirit makes intercession for me. Romans 8:26

41. I, _____,
know that God always knew me. Romans 8:29

42. I, _____,

have been given all things.
Romans 8:32

43. I, _____,
am inseparable from the love of God.
Romans 8:35

44. I, _____,
am more than a conqueror through
Christ. **Romans 8:37**

45. I, _____,
am God's temple. **I Corinthians 3:16-
17**

46. I, _____,

am washed, sanctified and justified by the Blood of Jesus. I Corinthians 6:11

47. I, _____,
have been bought with a price. I Corinthians 6:20

48. I, _____,
am the image and glory of God. I Corinthians 11:7

49. I, _____,
am triumphant in Christ. II Corinthians 2:14

50. I, _____,
am a sweet aroma manifesting the
presence of God wherever I go. II
Corinthians 2:14

51. I, _____,
am adequate for anything because my
adequacy comes from God.   II
Corinthians 3:5

52. I, _____,
am a new creation in Christ.   II
Corinthians 5:17

53. I, _____,
am an ambassador for Christ.   II

Corinthians 5:20

54. I, _____,
am strongest when I am weakest. II
Corinthians 12:10

55. I, _____,
am crucified with Christ and the life
I now live is His. Galatians 2:20

56. I, _____,
am redeemed from the curse of the
Law. Galatians 3:13

57. I, _____,
am filled with the fruit of the Spirit:

Love, joy, peace, long-suffering, gentleness, goodness, faith, meekness, temperance. Galatians 5:22-23

58. I,_____,
am in Christ Jesus. Ephesians 1:1

59. I,_____,
am blessed with every spiritual blessing. Ephesians 1:3

60. I,_____,
am chosen by God to be holy and blameless. Ephesians 1:4

61. I,_____,

am adopted by God through Jesus.
Ephesians 1:5

62. I,_____,
am accepted in the beloved.
Ephesians 1:6

63. I,_____,
have redemption through His blood.
Ephesians 1:7

64. I,_____,
am forgiven all my sins. Ephesians
1:7

65. I,_____,

have wisdom as I try to know His
will. Ephesians 1:8

66. I, _____,
know He has made known to me the
mystery of His will. Ephesians 1:9

67. I, _____,
am and have purpose according to
His plan. Ephesians 1:11

68. I, _____,
have obtained an inheritance.
Ephesians 1:11

69. I, _____,

am filled with the Holy Spirit of Promise. Ephesians 1:13

70. I, _____, have the spirit of wisdom and revelation of His knowledge. Ephesians 1:17

71. I, _____, know my eyes have been enlightened. Ephesians 1:18

72. I, _____, know the exceeding greatness of His power to me. Ephesians 1:19

73. I,_____,
know the hope of my calling.
Ephesians 1:18

74. I,_____,
know the riches of His inheritance in
the saints. Ephesians 1:18

75. I,_____,
am made alive with Christ.
Ephesians 2:1

76. I,_____,
am raised with Christ and seated in
the heavenlies. Ephesians 2:6

77. I, _____,
have been saved by grace through
faith. Ephesians 2:8

78. I, _____,
am God's handiwork created in
Christ Jesus under good works.
Ephesians 2:10

79. I, _____,
once afar off, am now made near by
the blood of Christ. Ephesians 2:13

80. I, _____,
have access through Jesus to the
Father. Ephesians 2:18

81. I, _____,
am a fellow citizen with the saints in
God's household. Ephesians 2:19

82. I, _____,
am built upon the foundation of the
apostles and Christ the chief
cornerstone. Ephesians 2:20

83. I, _____,
am able to walk boldly into Christ's
presence. Ephesians 3:12

84. I, _____,
do not have to be tossed about by
every wind of doctrine, the trickery of

men and their cunning craftiness.
Ephesians 3:16

**85. I, _____,
am strengthened with power through
His spirit of the inner man.
Ephesians 3:14**

**86. I, _____,
am receiving, exceeding, abundantly
above all that I ask or think.
Ephesians 3:20**

**87. I, _____,
can speak the truth in love and grow
up in all things under Him.**

Ephesians 4:15

88. I, _____,
have put off the old man. Ephesians
4:22

89. I, _____,
have been renewed in the spirit of my
mind. Ephesians 4:23

90. I, _____,
have put on the new man which was
created   according   to   God   in
righteousness   and   true   holiness.
Ephesians 4:24

91. I, _____ ,

once was darkness, but now I am

light in the Lord. Ephesians 5:8

92. I, _____ ,

am able to walk as a child of light.

Ephesians 5:8

93. I, _____ ,

am strong in the Lord and the power

of His might. Ephesians 6:10

94. I, _____ ,

choose to put on the whole armor of

God and stand. Ephesians 6:13

95. I, _____,
am able to quench all of Satan's
darts. Ephesians 6:16

96. I, _____,
know that it He who started a good
work in me will finish it. Philippians
1:6

97. I, _____,
will be ashamed in nothing, but with
all boldness, Christ will be magnified
in my body. Philippians 1:20

98. I, _____,
know for me to live is Christ, but to

die is gain. Philippians 1:21

99. I, _____,
know the mind which was in Christ is
in me. Philippians 2:5

100. I, _____,
know God is working in me both to
desire and to do His good pleasure.
Philippians 2:13

101. I, _____,
know my citizenship is in heaven
from which I eagerly await His
coming. Philippians 3:20

102. I, _____,
know He will transform my lowly
body to be conformed to His glorious
body. Philippians 3:21

103. I, _____,
can rejoice in the Lord always.
Philippians 4:4

SECTION III

NONE OTHER NAME

Jesus! Jesus! Jesus! Just to think that at this very name <u>every</u> knee shall bow and <u>every</u> tongue shall confess that He is, indeed, Lord. Oh, what a Lord we have - the very desire of nations and our very own Lord Jesus Christ. What a name for us to be associated with as joint-heirs with Christ in a world which only seems so out of control.

NONE OTHER NAME

Neither is there salvation in any other: for there is none other name under heaven given among men, whereby we must be saved. Acts 4:12

For the Son of man is come to seek and to save that which was lost. Luke 19:10

For all have sinned, and come short of the glory of God; Romans 3:23

But God commendeth his love toward us, in that, while we were yet sinners, Christ died for us. Romans 5:8

For the wages of sin is death; but the gift of God is eternal life through Jesus Christ our Lord. Romans 6:23

If we say that we have no sin, we deceive ourselves, and the truth is not in us. I John 1:8

I tell you, Nay: but, except ye repent, ye shall all likewise perish. Luke 13:3

Then Peter said unto them, Repent, and be baptized every one of you in the name of Jesus Christ for the remission of sins, and ye shall receive the gift of the Holy Ghost. For the promise is unto you, and to your children, and to all that are afar off, even as many as the Lord our God shall call. Acts 2:38-39

For by grace are ye saved through faith; and that not of yourselves: it is the gift of God: Not of works, lest any man should boast. Ephesians 2:8,9

If we confess our sins, he is faithful and just to forgive us our sins, and to cleanse us from all unrighteousness. I John 1:9

But if we walk in the light, as he is in the light, we have fellowship one with another, and the blood of Jesus

Christ his Son cleanseth us from all sin. I John 1:7

For with the heart man believeth unto righteousness; and with the mouth confession is made unto salvation. Romans 10:10

For God so loved the world, that he gave his only begotten Son, that whosoever believeth in him should not perish, but have everlasting life. John 3:16

Verily, verily, I say unto you, He that believeth on me hath everlasting life. John 6:47

But as many as received him, to them gave he power to become the sons of God, even to them that believe on his name: John 1:12

That if thou shalt confess with thy mouth the Lord Jesus, and shalt believe in thine heart that God hath raised him from the dead, thou shalt be saved. For whosoever shall call upon the name of the Lord shall be saved. Romans 10:9,13

And ye shall know the truth, and the truth shall make you free. John 8:32

SECTION IV

BLESSED ARE . . .

How blessed we are. The Scriptures use this very term to tell us that we <u>are</u> special and we <u>are</u> His people. When we consider these words and apply them to our lives, we find that we truly <u>are</u> blessed by our Lord. It is, of course, up to us to accept Christ's blessings on our lives, but He has freely given us all that He is and, we <u>are</u> blessed.

BLESSED ARE THE POOR IN
SPIRIT FOR THEIRS IS
THE KINGDOM OF HEAVEN

Though the LORD be high, yet hath he respect unto the lowly: but the proud he knoweth afar off. Psalm 138:6

Surely he scorneth the scorners: but he giveth grace unto the lowly. Proverbs 3:34

And the publican, standing afar off, would not lift up so much as his eyes unto heaven, but smote upon his breast, saying, God be merciful to me

a sinner. I tell you, this man went down to his house justified rather than the other: for every one that exalteth himself shall be abased; and he that humbleth himself shall be exalted. Luke 18:13-14

Humble yourselves in the sight of the Lord, and he shall lift you up. James 4:10

Humble yourselves therefore under the mighty hand of God, that he may exalt you in due time: Casting all your care upon him; for he careth for you. I Peter 5:6-7

When pride cometh, then cometh shame: but with the lowly is wisdom. Proverbs 11:2

For thus saith the high and lofty One that inhabiteth eternity, whose name is Holy; I dwell in the high and holy place, with him also that is of a contrite and humble spirit, to revive the spirit of the humble, and to revive the heart of the contrite ones. Isaiah 57:15

But he giveth more grace. Wherefore he saith, God resisteth the proud, but giveth grace unto the humble. James 4:6

LORD, thou hast heard the desire of the humble: thou wilt prepare their heart, thou wilt cause thine ear to hear: To judge the fatherless and the oppressed, that the man of the earth may no more oppress. Psalm 10:17,18

A man's pride shall bring him low: but honour shall uphold the humble in spirit. Proverbs 29:23

BLESSED ARE THEY THAT MOURN; FOR THEY SHALL BE COMFORTED

But Jesus turned him about, and when he saw her, he said, Daughter, be of good comfort; thy faith hath made thee whole. And the woman was made whole from that hour. Matthew 9:22

For whatsoever things were written aforetime were written for our learning, that we through patience and comfort of the scriptures might have hope. Romans 15:4

But he that prophesieth speaketh unto men to edification, and exhortation, and comfort. I Corinthians 14:3

Blessed be God, even the Father of our Lord Jesus Christ, the Father of mercies, and the God of all comfort; II Corinthians 1:3

So that contrariwise ye ought rather to forgive him, and comfort him, lest perhaps such a one should be swallowed up with overmuch sorrow. II Corinthains 2:7

Yea, though I walk through the valley of the shadow of death, I will fear no evil: for thou art with me; thy rod and thy staff they comfort me. Psalm 23:4

Thou shalt increase my greatness, and comfort me on every side. Psalm 71:21

For the LORD shall comfort Zion: he will comfort all her waste places; and he will make her wilderness like Eden, and her desert like the garden of the LORD; joy and gladness shall be found therein, thanksgiving, and the voice of melody. Isaiah 51:3

Finally, brethren, farewell. Be perfect, be of good comfort, be of one mind, live in peace; and the God of love and peace shall be with you. II Corinthains 13:11

And I will pray the Father, and he shall give you another Comforter, that he may abide with you for ever; John 14:16

I will not leave you comfortless: I will come to you. Yet a little while, and the world seeth me no more; but ye see me: because I live, ye shall live also. John 14:18-19

BLESSED ARE THE MEEK:
FOR THEY SHALL INHERIT
THE EARTH.

The meek will he guide in judgment: and the meek will he teach his way. Psalm 25:9

But the meek shall inherit the earth; and shall delight themselves in the abundance of peace. Psalm 37:11

The LORD lifteth up the meek: he casteth the wicked down to the ground. Psalm 147:6

For the LORD taketh pleasure in his people: he will beautify the meek with salvation. Psalm 149:4

Seek ye the LORD, all ye meek of the earth, which have wrought his judgment; seek righteousness, seek meekness: it may be ye shall be hid in the day of the LORD'S anger. Zephaniah 2:3

Take my yoke upon you, and learn of me; for I am meek and lowly in heart: and ye shall find rest unto your souls. Matthew 11:29

By humility and the fear of the LORD are riches, and honour, and life. Proverbs 22:4

A soft answer turneth away wrath: but grievous words stir up anger. Proverbs 15:1

*BLESSED ARE THEY THAT
HUNGER AND THIRST
AFTER RIGHTEOUSNESS:
FOR THEY SHALL BE FILLED.*

But if from thence thou shalt seek the LORD thy God, thou shalt find him, if thou seek him with all thy heart and with all thy soul. Deuteronomy 4:29

And they that know thy name will put their trust in thee: for thou, LORD, hast not forsaken them that seek thee. Psalm 9:10

I love them that love me; and those

that seek me early shall find me.
Proverbs 8:17

And ye shall seek me, and find me,
when ye shall search for me with all
your heart. Jeremiah 29:13

(For after all these things do the
Gentiles seek:) for your heavenly
Father knoweth that ye have need of
all these things. But seek ye first the
kingdom of God, and his righteousness; and all these things shall
be added unto you. Matthew 6:32-33

And I say unto you, Ask, and it
shall be given you; seek, and ye shall
find; knock, and it shall be opened
unto you. For every one that asketh
receiveth; and he that seeketh
findeth; and to him that knocketh it

shall be opened. If a son shall ask bread of any of you that is a father, will he give him a stone? or if he ask a fish, will he for a fish give him a serpent? Or if he shall ask an egg, will he offer him a scorpion? If ye then, being evil, know how to give good gifts unto your children: how much more shall your heavenly Father give the Holy Spirit to them that ask him? Luke 11:9-13

And seek not ye what ye shall eat, or what ye shall drink, neither be ye of doubtful mind. For all these things do the nations of the world seek after: and your Father knoweth that ye have need of these things. But rather seek ye the kingdom of God; and all these things shall be added unto you. Fear not, little flock; for it is your Father's good pleasure to give you the kingdom. Luke 12:29-32

If ye then be risen with Christ, seek those things which are above, where Christ sitteth on the right hand of God. Set your affection on things above, not on things on the earth. For ye are dead, and your life is hid with Christ in God. When Christ, who is our life, shall appear, then shall ye also appear with him in glory. Colossians 3:1-4

But whosoever drinketh of the water that I shall give him shall never thirst; but the water that I shall give him shall be in him a well of water springing up into everlasting life. John 4:14

Search me, O God, and know my heart: try me, and know my thoughts. Psalm 139:23

And Jesus said unto them, I am the bread of life: he that cometh to me shall never hunger; and he that believeth on me shall never thirst. John 6:35

All that the Father giveth me shall come to me; and him that cometh to me I will in no wise cast out. For I came down from heaven, not to do mine own will, but the will of him that sent me. And this is the Father's will which hath sent me, that of all which he hath given me I should lose nothing, but should raise it up again at the last day. John 6:37-39

BLESSED ARE THE MERCIFUL: FOR THEY SHALL OBTAIN MERCY.

(For the **LORD** thy God is a merciful God;) he will not forsake thee, neither destroy thee, nor forget the covenant of thy fathers which he sware unto them. **Deuteronomy 4:31**

He is ever merciful, and lendeth; and his seed is blessed. **Psalm 37:26**

The **LORD** is merciful and gracious, slow to anger, and plenteous in mercy. **Psalm 103:8**

Be ye therefore merciful, as your Father also is merciful. Judge not, and ye shall not be judged: condemn not, and ye shall not be condemned: forgive, and ye shall be forgiven: Give, and it shall be given unto you; good measure, pressed down, and shaken together, and running over, shall men give into your bosom. For with the same measure that ye mete withal it shall be measured to you again. Luke 6:36-38

And he said, LORD God of Israel, there is no God like thee, in heaven above, or on earth beneath, who keepest covenant and mercy with thy servants that walk before thee with all their heart: I Kings 8:23

Not by works of righteousness which we have done, but according to his mercy he saved us, by the washing of regeneration, and renewing of the Holy Ghost; Which he shed on us abundantly through Jesus Christ our Saviour; That being justified by his grace, we should be made heirs according to the hope of eternal life. Titus 3:5-7

But thou, O Lord, art a God full of compassion, and gracious, longsuffering, and plenteous in mercy and truth. Psalm 86:15

So Jesus had compassion on them, and touched their eyes: and immediately their eyes received sight, and they followed him. Matthew 20:34

BLESSED ARE THE PURE IN HEART: FOR THEY SHALL SEE GOD.

Seeing ye have purified your souls in obeying the truth through the Spirit unto unfeigned love of the brethren, see that ye love one another with a pure heart fervently: Being born again, not of corruptible seed, but of incorruptible, by the word of God, which liveth and abideth for ever. I Peter 1:22-23

Blessed is the man unto whom the LORD imputeth not iniquity, and in whose spirit there is no guile. Psalm 32:2

Nathanael saith unto him, Whence knowest thou me? Jesus answered and said unto him, Before that Philip called thee, when thou wast under the fig tree, I saw thee. Nathanael answered and saith unto him, Rabbi, thou art the Son of God; thou art the King of Israel. Jesus answered and said unto him, Because I said unto thee, I saw thee under the fig tree, believest thou? thou shalt see greater things than these. And he saith unto him, Verily, verily, I say unto you, Hereafter ye shall see heaven open, and the angels of God ascending and descending upon the Son of man. John 1:48-51

For he that will love life, and see good days, let him refrain his tongue from evil, and his lips that they speak no guile: Let him eschew evil, and do good; let him seek peace, and ensue it. For the eyes of the Lord are over the righteous, and his ears are open unto their prayers: but the face of the Lord is against them that do evil. I Peter 3:10-12

He that hath clean hands, and a pure heart; who hath not lifted up his soul unto vanity, nor sworn deceitfully. He shall receive the blessing from the LORD, and righteousness from the God of his salvation. Psalm 24:4-5

Finally, brethren, whatsoever things are true, whatsoever things are honest, whatsoever things are just, whatsoever things are pure, whatsoever things are lovely, whatsoever things are of good report; if there be any virtue, and if there be any praise, think on these things. Those things, which ye have both learned, and received, and heard, and seen in me, do: and the God of peace shall be with you. Philippians 4:8-9

LORD, who shall abide in thy tabernacle? who shall dwell in thy holy hill? He that walketh uprightly, and worketh righteousness, and speaketh the truth in his heart. He that backbiteth not with his tongue, nor doeth evil to his neighbour, nor taketh up a reproach against his neighbour. Psalm 15:1-3

Truly God is good to Israel, even to such as are of a clean heart. Psalm 73:1

BLESSED ARE THE PEACEMAKERS: FOR THEY SHALL BE CALLED THE CHILDREN OF GOD.

The Spirit itself beareth witness with our spirit, that we are the children of God: And if children, then heirs; heirs of God, and joint-heirs with Christ; if so be that we suffer with him, that we may be also glorified together. Romans 8:16-17

Whosoever believeth that Jesus is the Christ is born of God: and every one that loveth him that begat loveth him also that is begotten of him. By this we know that we love the children of God, when we love God, and keep his commandments. For this is the love of God, that we keep his commandments: and his commandments are not grievous. For whatsoever is born of God overcometh the world: and this is the victory that overcometh the world, even our faith. I John 5:1-4

Fret not thyself because of evildoers, neither be thou envious against the workers of iniquity. For they shall soon be cut down like the grass, and wither as the green herb. Trust in the LORD, and do good; so shalt thou dwell in the land, and verily thou shalt be fed. Delight thyself also in the LORD; and he shall give thee the desires of thine heart. Commit thy way unto the LORD; trust also in him; and he shall bring it to pass. Psalm 37:1-5

Peace I leave with you, my peace I

give unto you: not as the world giveth, give I unto you. Let not your heart be troubled, neither let it be afraid. John 14:27

The LORD will give strength unto his people; the LORD will bless his people with peace. Psalm 29:11

When a man's ways please the LORD, he maketh even his enemies to be at peace with him. Proverbs 16:7

There remaineth therefore a rest to the people of God. Hebrews 4:9

Behold, what manner of love the Father hath bestowed upon us, that we should be called the sons of God:

therefore the world knoweth us not, because it knew him not. Beloved, now are we the sons of God, and it doth not yet appear what we shall be: but we know that, when he shall appear, we shall be like him; for we shall see him as he is. And every man that hath this hope in him purifieth himself, even as he is pure. I John 3:1-3

And the fruit of righteousness is sown in peace of them that make peace. James 3:18

BLESSED ARE THEY WHICH ARE PERSECUTED FOR RIGHTEOUS- NESS' SAKE: FOR THEIRS IS THE KINGDOM OF HEAVEN.

Blessed are ye, when men shall revile you, and persecute you, and shall say all manner of evil against you falsely, for my sake. Rejoice, and be exceeding glad: for great is your reward in heaven: for so persecuted they the prophets which were before you. Matthew 5:11-12

Beloved, think it not strange concerning the fiery trial which is to try you, as though some strange thing happened unto you: But rejoice, inasmuch as ye are partakers of

Christ's sufferings; that, when his glory shall be revealed, ye may be glad also with exceeding joy. I Peter 4:12-13

We are troubled on every side, yet not distressed; we are perplexed, but not in despair; Persecuted, but not forsaken; cast down, but not destroyed; Always bearing about in the body the dying of the Lord Jesus, that the life also of Jesus might be made manifest in our body. II Corinthians 4:8-10

But I say unto you, Love your enemies, bless them that curse you, do good to them that hate you, and pray for them which despitefully use you, and persecute you; That ye may be the children of your Father which is in heaven: Matthew 5:44-45a

And fear not them which kill the body, but are not able to kill the soul: but rather fear him which is able to destroy both soul and body in hell. Matthew 10:28

Whosoever therefore shall confess me before men, him will I confess also before my Father which is in heaven. Matthew 10:32

He that overcometh shall inherit all things; and I will be his God, and he shall be my son. Revelation 21:7

Fear none of those things which thou shalt suffer: behold, the devil shall cast some of you into prison, that ye may be tried; and ye shall have tribulation ten days: be thou faithful unto death, and I will give thee a crown of life. Revelation 2:10

SECTION V

THE FRUIT OF THE SPIRIT IS . . .

Fruit! What is fruit? Fruit is that natural product which comes from a living, functioning and growing creation. We are told in scriptures to "be like a tree planted by the rivers of living waters" and as such, we, too, produce fruit as a living, functioning and growing creation of God. It is the Spirit of God within us which brings forth His fruit through us.

LOVE

The LORD preserveth all them that love him: but all the wicked will he destroy. Psalm 145:20

I love them that love me; and those that seek me early shall find me. Proverbs 8:17

Hatred stirreth up strifes: but love covereth all sins. Proverbs 10:12

Jesus said unto him, Thou shalt

love the Lord thy God with all thy
heart, and with all thy soul, and with
all thy mind. This is the first and
great commandment. And the second
is like unto it, Thou shalt love thy
neighbour as thyself. Matthew 22:37-
39

For God so loved the world, that he
gave his only begotten Son, that
whosoever believeth in him should not
perish, but have everlasting life.
John 3:16

A new commandment I give unto
you, That ye love one another; as I
have loved you, that ye also love one
another. John 13:34

If ye love me, keep my
commandments. John 14:15

Blessed is the man that endureth temptation: for when he is tried, he shall receive the crown of life, which the Lord hath promised to them that love him. James 1:12

And we know that all things work together for good to them that love God, to them who are the called according to his purpose. Romans 8:28

But if any man love God, the same is known of him. I Corinthians 8:3

JOY

Thou wilt shew me the path of life: in thy presence is fulness of joy; at thy right hand there are pleasures for evermore. Psalm 16:11

They that sow in tears shall reap in joy. Psalm 126:5

Therefore the redeemed of the LORD shall return, and come with singing unto Zion; and everlasting joy shall be upon their head: they shall obtain gladness and joy; and sorrow and mourning shall flee away. Isaiah 51:11

These things have I spoken unto you, that my joy might remain in you, and that your joy might be full. John 15:11

And ye now therefore have sorrow: but I will see you again, and your heart shall rejoice, and your joy no man taketh from you. And in that day ye shall ask me nothing. Verily, verily, I say unto you, Whatsoever ye shall ask the Father in my name, he will give it you. Hitherto have ye asked nothing in my name: ask, and ye shall receive, that your joy may be full. John 16:22-24

For the kingdom of God is not meat and drink; but righteousness, and peace, and joy in the Holy Ghost. Romans 14:17

PEACE

The LORD will give strength unto his people; the LORD will bless his people with peace. Psalm 29:11

Great peace have they which love thy law: and nothing shall offend them. Psalm 119:165

Peace I leave with you, my peace I give unto you: I go away, and come again unto you. John 14:27a

Deceit is in the heart of them that

imagine evil: but to the counsellors of peace is joy. Proverbs 12:20

And the work of righteousness shall be peace; and the effect of righteousness quietness and assurance for ever. Isaiah 32:17

And the peace of God, which passeth all understanding, shall keep your hearts and minds through Christ Jesus. Philippians 4:7

Now no chastening for the present seemeth to be joyous, but grievous: nevertheless afterward it yieldeth the peaceable fruit of righteousness unto them which are exercised thereby. Hebrews 12:11

Follow peace with all men, and holiness, without which no man shall see the Lord: Hebrews 12:14

LONGSUFFERING

But thou, O Lord, art a God full of compassion, and gracious, longsuffering, and plenteous in mercy and truth.Psalm 86:15

In your patience possess ye your souls. Luke 21:19

To them who by patient continuance in well doing seek for glory and honour and immortality, eternal life: Romans 2:7

For this cause we also, since the day we heard it, do not cease to pray for you, and to desire that ye might be filled with the knowledge of his will in all wisdom and spiritual understanding; That ye might walk worthy of the Lord unto all pleasing, being fruitful in every good work, and increasing in the knowledge of God; Strengthened with all might, according to his glorious power, unto all patience and longsuffering with joyfulness; Giving thanks unto the Father, which hath made us meet to be partakers of the inheritance of the saints in light: Who hath delivered us from the power of darkness, and hath translated us into the kingdom of his dear Son: Colossians 1:9-13

Howbeit for this cause I obtained mercy, that in me first Jesus Christ might shew forth all longsuffering, for a pattern to them which should hereafter believe on him to life everlasting. I Timothy 1:16

Take, my brethren, the prophets, who have spoken in the name of the Lord, for an example of suffering affliction, and of patience. Behold, we count them happy which endure. James 5:10-11a

The Lord is not slack concerning his promise, as some men count slackness; but is longsuffering to us-ward, not willing that any should perish, but that all should come to repentance. II Peter 3:9

Seeing then that all these things shall be dissolved, what manner of persons ought ye to be in all holy conversation and godliness, II Peter 3:11

GENTLENESS

Thou hast also given me the shield of thy salvation: and thy gentleness hath made me great. II Samuel 22:36

But the wisdom that is from above is first pure, then peaceable, gentle, and easy to be intreated, full of mercy and good fruits, without partiality, and without hypocrisy. James 3:17

And be ye kind one to another,

tenderhearted, forgiving one another, even as God for Christ's sake hath forgiven you. Ephesians 4:32

Be ye therefore followers of God, as dear children; And walk in love, as Christ also hath loved us, and hath given himself for us an offering and a sacrifice to God for a sweetsmelling savour. Ephesians 5:1-2

And beside this, giving all diligence, add to your faith virtue; and to virtue knowledge; And to knowledge temperance; and to temperance patience; and to patience godliness; And to godliness brotherly kindness; and to brotherly kindness charity. For if these things be in you, and abound, they make you that ye shall neither be barren nor unfruitful in the knowledge of our Lord Jesus Christ. II Peter 1:5-8

GOODNESS

And thou shalt do that which is right and good in the sight of the LORD: that it may be well with thee, and that thou mayest go in and possess the good land which the LORD sware unto thy fathers, Deuteronomy 6:18

And now, LORD, thou art God, and hast promised this goodness unto thy servant: Now therefore let it please thee to bless the house of thy servant, that it may be before thee for ever: for thou blessest, O LORD, and it shall be blessed for ever. I Chronicles 17:26-27

Surely goodness and mercy shall follow me all the days of my life: and I will dwell in the house of the LORD for ever. Psalm 23:6

Trust in the LORD, and do good; so shalt thou dwell in the land, and verily thou shalt be fed. Psalm 37:3

The steps of a good man are ordered by the LORD: and he delighteth in his way. Though he fall, he shall not be utterly cast down: for the LORD upholdeth him with his hand. Psalm 37:23-24

And he said unto him, Thy prayers and thine alms are come up for a memorial before God. Acts 10:4b

And let us not be weary in well doing: for in due season we shall reap, if we faint not. Galatians 6:9

And the world passeth away, and the lust thereof: but he that doeth the will of God abideth for ever. I John 2:17

FAITH

A faithful man shall abound with blessings: but he that maketh haste to be rich shall not be innocent. Proverbs 28:20

And, behold, they brought to him a man sick of the palsy, lying on a bed: and Jesus seeing their faith said unto the sick of the palsy; Son, be of good cheer; thy sins be forgiven thee. Matthew 9:2

But Jesus turned him about, and

when he saw her, he said, Daughter, be of good comfort; thy faith hath made thee whole. And the woman was made whole from that hour. Matthew 9:22

Then touched he their eyes, saying, According to your faith be it unto you. Matthew 9:29

Knowing that a man is not justified by the works of the law, but by the faith of Jesus Christ, even we have believed in Jesus Christ, that we might be justified by the faith of Christ, and not by the works of the law: for by the works of the law shall no flesh be justified. Galatians 2:16

I am crucified with Christ: nevertheless I live; yet not I, but

Christ liveth in me: and the life which I now live in the flesh I live by the faith of the Son of God, who loved me, and gave himself for me. Galatians 2:20

;. . . that we might receive the promise of the Spirit through faith. Galatians 3:14b

For ye are all the children of God by faith in Christ Jesus. Galatians 3:26

Now faith is the substance of things hoped for, the evidence of things not seen. For by it the elders obtained a good report. Through faith we understand that the worlds were framed by the word of God, so that things which are seen were not made of things which do appear. Hebrews 11:1-3

MEEKNESS

Seek ye the LORD, all ye meek of the earth, which have wrought his judgment; seek righteousness, seek meekness: it may be ye shall be hid in the day of the LORD'S anger.
Zephaniah 2:3

Whosoever therefore shall break one of these least commandments, and shall teach men so, he shall be called the least in the kingdom of heaven: but whosoever shall do and teach them, the same shall be called

great in the kingdom of heaven.
Matthew 5:19

He that findeth his life shall lose it: and he that loseth his life for my sake shall find it. Matthew 10:39

But let it be the hidden man of the heart, in that which is not corruptible, even the ornament of a meek and quiet spirit, which is in the sight of God of great price. I Peter 3:4

But sanctify the Lord God in your hearts: and be ready always to give an answer to every man that asketh you a reason of the hope that is in you with meekness and fear: Having a good conscience; that, whereas they speak evil of you, as of evildoers, they may be ashamed that falsely accuse your good conversation in Christ. For it is better, if the will of God be so, that ye suffer for well doing, than for evil doing. I Peter 3:15-17

The spirit of the Lord God is upon me; because the Lord hath anointed me to preach good tidings unto the meek; he hath sent me to bind up the broken-hearted, to proclaim liberty to the captives, and the opening of the prison to them that are bound; To proclaim the acceptable year of the Lord, and the day of vengeance of our God; to comfort all that mourn; To appoint unto them that mourn in Zion, to give unto them beauty for ashes, the oil of joy for mourning, the garment of praise for the spirit of heaviness; that they might be called trees of righteousness, the planting of the Lord, that he might be glorified. Isaiah 61:1-3

TEMPERANCE

A little that a righteous man hath is better than the riches of many wicked. Psalm 37:16

And every man that striveth for the mastery is temperate in all things. Now they do it to obtain a corruptible crown; but we an incorruptible. I Corinthians 9:25

Let your moderation be known unto all men. The Lord is at hand. Philippians 4:5

And the peace of God, which passeth all understanding, shall keep your hearts and minds through Christ Jesus. Philippians 4:7

. . . But a lover of hospitality, a lover of good men, sober, just, holy, temperate; Holding fast the faithful word as he hath been taught, that he may be able by sound doctrine both to exhort and to convince the gainsayers. Titus 1:8-9

Young men likewise exhort to be sober minded. In all things shewing thyself a pattern of good works: in doctrine shewing uncorruptness, gravity, sincerity, Sound speech, that cannot be condemned; that he that is of the contrary part may be ashamed, having no evil thing to say of you. Titus 2:6-8

Be sober, be vigilant; because your adversary the devil, as a roaring lion, walketh about, seeking whom he may devour: I Peter 5:8

But the God of all grace, who hath called us unto his eternal glory by Christ Jesus, after that ye have suffered a while, make you perfect, stablish, strengthen, settle you. I Peter 5:10

For if these things be in you, and abound, they make you that ye shall neither be barren nor unfruitful in the knowledge of our Lord Jesus Christ. II Peter 1:8

SECTION VI

YOU <u>SHALL</u> RECEIVE POWER

God has promised us power! He did not say that <u>maybe</u> we would receive power, but rather He said we <u>shall</u> receive power. Power is something which, then, is ours as a gift from God, but it is up to each of us to accept that power and adapt this very special gift to our lives on a daily basis. If we don't, the power remains unused and unnoticed.

POWER

But ye shall receive power, after that the Holy Ghost is come upon you: and ye shall be witnesses unto me both in Jerusalem, and in all Judaea, and in Samaria, and unto the uttermost part of the earth. Acts 1:8

I indeed baptize you with water unto repentance: but he that cometh after me is mightier than I, whose shoes I am not worthy to bear: he shall baptize you with the Holy Ghost, and with fire: Matthew 3:11

Wherefore I say unto you, All manner of sin and blasphemy shall be forgiven unto men: but the blasphemy against the Holy Ghost shall not be forgiven unto men. Matthew 12:31

For the Holy Ghost shall teach you in the same hour what ye ought to say. Luke 12:12

But the Comforter, which is the Holy Ghost, whom the Father will send in my name, he shall teach you all things, and bring all things to your remembrance, whatsoever I have said unto you. John 14:26

And they were all filled with the Holy Ghost, and began to speak with other tongues, as the Spirit gave them utterance. Acts 2:4

And now, Lord, behold their threatenings: and grant unto thy servants, that with all boldness they may speak thy word, By stretching forth thine hand to heal; and that signs and wonders may be done by the name of thy holy child Jesus. And when they had prayed, the place was shaken where they were assembled together; and they were all filled with the Holy Ghost, and they spake the word of God with boldness. Acts 4:29-31

How God anointed Jesus of Nazareth with the Holy Ghost and with power: who went about doing good, and healing all that were oppressed of the devil; for God was with him. And we are witnesses of all things which he did both in the land of the Jews, and in Jerusalem; whom they slew and hanged on a tree: Him

God raised up the third day, and shewed him openly; Not to all the people, but unto witnesses chosen before of God, even to us, who did eat and drink with him after he rose from the dead. And he commanded us to preach unto the people, and to testify that it is he which was ordained of God to be the Judge of quick and dead. To him give all the prophets witness, that through his name whosoever believeth in him shall receive remission of sins. While Peter yet spake these words, the Holy Ghost fell on all them which heard the word. And they of the circumcision which believed were astonished, as many as came with Peter, because that on the Gentiles also was poured out the gift of the Holy Ghost. For they heard them speak with tongues, and magnify God. Then answered Peter, Can any man forbid water, that these should not be baptized, which have received the Holy Ghost as well as we? And he commanded them to be baptized in the name of the Lord. Then prayed they him to tarry certain days. Acts 10:38-48

Then remembered I the word of the Lord, how that he said, John indeed baptized with water; but ye shall be baptized with the Holy Ghost. Acts 11:16

For the kingdom of God is not meat and drink; but righteousness, and peace, and joy in the Holy Ghost. Romans 14:17

Now the God of hope fill you with all joy and peace in believing, that ye may abound in hope, through the power of the Holy Ghost. Romans 15:13

Now concerning spiritual gifts, brethren, I would not have you ignorant. I Corinthains 12:1

But the manifestation of the Spirit is given to every man to profit withal. For to one is given by the Spirit the word of wisdom; to another the word of knowledge by the same Spirit; To another faith by the same Spirit; to another the gifts of healing by the same Spirit; To another the working of miracles; to another prophecy; to another discerning of spirits; to another divers kinds of tongues; to another the interpretation of tongues: But all these worketh that one and the selfsame Spirit, dividing to every man severally as he will. I

Now ye are the body of Christ, and members in particular. And God hath set some in the church, first apostles, secondarily prophets, thirdly teachers, after that miracles, then gifts of healings, helps, governments, diversities of tongues. I Corinthians 12:27-28

Not by works of righteousness which we have done, but according to his mercy he saved us, by the washing of regeneration, and renewing of the Holy Ghost; Which he shed on us abundantly through Jesus Christ our Saviour; Titus 3:5-6

For the prophecy came not in old time by the will of man: but holy men of God spake as they were moved by the Holy Ghost. II Peter 1:21

But ye, beloved, building up yourselves on your most holy faith, praying in the Holy Ghost, Keep yourselves in the love of God, looking for the mercy of our Lord Jesus Christ unto eternal life. Jude 1:20-21

But as many as received him, to them gave he power to become the sons of God, even to them that believe on his name: Which were born, not of blood, nor of the will of the flesh, nor of the will of man, but of God. John 1:12-13

For I am not ashamed of the gospel of Christ: for it is the power of God unto salvation to every one that believeth; to the Jew first, and also to the Greek. Romans 1:16

Let every soul be subject unto the higher powers. For there is no power but of God: the powers that be are ordained of God. Romans 13:1

EPILOGUE

SERENITY in times of question, trouble, uncertainty, fear or calamity of any kind is ours as believers in Jesus Christ our Lord. In these days of turmoil, it appears that we have no hope, but Jesus tells us to "be of good cheer, for I have overcome the world." These foregoing promises and outline as to our position in Jesus Christ because of

His life, death and resurrection are the certainty which we need in such times.

Of course, all these promises are for those who have been born again by the grace of God. As the scriptures tells us: "For all have sinned and come short of the glory of God" and "The wages of sin is death, but the gift of God is eternal life through Jesus Christ our Lord." If you have not accepted this gift, then it is our prayer that you, right now, call upon the Giver of this gift and simply ask Him to forgive you for your sins and accept Jesus as your personal Savior, His perfect gift to you.

Once you have done this, share your decision with someone else who has received this wonderful gift and ask them to help you learn more from His word as to the promises which are now yours from our Father.

Look for these Convenient
DUGAN
HANDYBOOK Titles

- Everything You Need to Know About Social Security

- The Consumers' Amortization Guide

- The Dugan Bible Dictionary

- The Cruden's Condensed Concordance

- Daily Prayer Journal

- Bible Stories from the Book of Acts

- Journals

- Bible Questions and Answers

- Precious Promises